Sketching Indoors

Sketching Indoors

SHARON FINMARK

CASSELL

LONDON

To Moyra, Peter, Marcus and Louise with thanks.

First published in the United Kingdom in 1999 by Cassell

Distributed in the United States by
Sterling Publishing Co. Inc.
387 Park Avenue South
New York NY 10016-8810

A CIP record for this book is available from the British Library

ISBN 0-304-35210-1

Edited by Caroline Ball

Printed and bound in Great Britain

Cassell
Illustrated Division
The Orion Publishing Group
Wellington House,
125 Strand
London WC2R 0BB

Contents

Introduction

Everyone interested in painting and drawing needs to keep a sketchbook. Why? To start with, a sketchbook is invaluable for practicing different methods of work, for trying out various materials – pencil, ink, charcoal – or for refining drawing techniques – shape and form, wash and line, tones. Use a sketchbook for putting down information wherever you might be and it becomes an invaluable source of information at a later date, almost like a catalogue of ideas and memories to dip into. Details and sketches recorded in it are a great stimulus for, say, a finished painting, indispensible visual tools for working out the most satisfying plan or design for a more developed work.

Sketches are personal impressions; they should be done exclusively for your own pleasure and interest. With this in mind, sketching indoors has several plus factors. There is the comfort of not worrying about the weather, which can be a real drawback to sketching out of doors. If you are at home, there is the convenience of having all the equipment to hand – that very special pencil may just be upstairs, rather than an hour's journey away. And, especially for the beginner, there is not the daunting prospect of whipping out your sketchbook in public, attracting the comments and critical glances of strangers.

A portable sketchbook is convenient enough to take anywhere – cafés, historic houses, on holiday, to work – but, as the following pages show,

there are countless opportunities for inspiration behind our own front doors. First, however, a little preparation of tools and equipment.

Materials and marks

Whatever the circumstances, a sketch is a very direct response to a scene or a moment, and whereas a finished drawing or painting may be carefully worked and detailed – perhaps more contrived – a sketch should be unlaboured. This means using tools that are best suited to the occasion and to you.

All tools have drawbacks and capabilities. Understanding what each of them can offer and gaining technical confidence in them will only come with practice, but will enhance your ability to gather visual information from the world around you. Technically you need to be flexible, so that you can respond immediately to the circumstances – the light might be changing, you may have a limit on your time – and familiarity and proficiency with a variety of different materials will enable you to work with the appropriate medium. A ball-point pen is fast to work with, a brush slower, although of course both can be used leisurely or swiftly, depending on what the situation demands.

All the sketches in this book are monochrome, but if colour is going to be a factor later, you can write colour notes on a line sketch made in pencil, ink or charcoal to jog your memory of what you have observed.

Sketchbooks

Sketchbooks come in all forms and sizes, each having their own uses and advantages.

Perhaps the most useful to begin with is a standard sketchbook of smooth cartridge paper – 15 × 10 cm (6 × 4 in) is a handy pocket size. Spiral-bound books mean that sheets can easily be torn out; sewn or glued bindings mean that you can choose to work right across the double-page spread.

Probably the most important thing to remember when considering paper is its texture, and the medium you are going to be using. Generally speaking, smooth, hard paper is used for pen and pencil work, rougher surfaces for charcoal, conte, pastels, crayons and soft pencils. Rougher-textured paper can also be used for wet media, such as ink washes, watercolour and water-soluble pencils.

Watercolour paper comes in its own selection of colours and finishes. Hot press is smooth, and best for fine detail. Rough is, as its name implies, more heavily textured. Not is somewhere in between. Ingres is lightly textured paper, made in endless colours, and is ideal for soft pencil and pastel work.

Keep your sketchbooks to look at in the future. You will be surprised by how they will remind you of old ideas and trigger off new ones.

Pencils

All pencils are graded in degrees of H (hardness) or B (softness). I would suggest HB or 2B as the most useful. 4B and 6B are very soft, and excellent for expressing tone, shape and form (see page 9 for how different shading effects can be produced). You can also get water-soluble pencils. By adding a touch of water, these produce a transparent wash, so with just one drawing tool you can achieve both line and tone.

Charcoal and charcoal pencils

Charcoal is a very versatile material, and especially useful when you are just starting out, as it pushes you to treat the subject in broad terms rather than getting too bogged down in detail. Charcoal is also very easy to blend and smudge to create tone; you can also correct merely by rubbing marks off with your finger or a tissue. However, its softness means that it is inclined to go everywhere and will need fixing once the sketch is finished (all art shops stock charcoal fixative).

Charcoal sticks are sold in packs – for sketching the finer size is advisable as the fatter sticks will make cruder, broader marks more suited to larger-scale work. Charcoal pencils are made of compressed charcoal, which means they are cleaner to handle and have a harder mark.

Clutch pencil

2B   3B   4B   5B   6B pencils

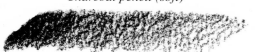

Charcoal pencil (soft)

Water-soluble pencil

Charcoal pencil (light)

Brush pen with cartridge

Art pen

Charcoal pencil (medium)

Conte pencil (medium)

Conte pencil (soft)

Brush and black watercolour paint

Conte sticks

Fine felt-tipped pen

Clutch pencil

3B pencil

2B pencil

4B pencil

5B pencil   *6B pencil*

Brush pen

Art pen

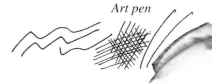

Brush and black watercolour paint

Fine felt-tipped pen

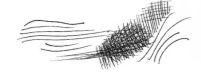

Shading with pencil

Adding shading to give tone and depth to a sketch is looked at later on (see pages 28–31), but right from the beginning get a feel for how different pencils shade. Drawing roughly parallel lines very close together is called hatching. Hatching can be straight and mechanical or free and sketchy and at any angle from horizontal to vertical. Going over a first layer of hatching with another at right angles is cross-hatching and of course gives deeper shading. By changing direction often you can produce a mesh of tone – always proceed slowly and build up to denser, darker areas.

The other way to show shading – and personally I find it less laborious – is to use the side of the pencil drawn broadly across the paper, again starting with lighter strokes and increasing the pressure for darker areas. You can blend marks with a finger or with an eraser, and with water-soluble pencils produce a light wash.

Conte and pastels

Conte is a hard version of chalk and, like charcoal, also comes in pencil form. Pastels, which come in many colours, are available as sticks or pencils. In pencil form, both are ideal for creating fine lines for delicate blending, as they can be sharpened to a point.

Pens, inks and brushes

Forget dip pens; they are too messy. You can achieve the same effect with sketch pens; these come in a cartridge fountain pen format with a flexible nib.

Ordinary fibre-tipped pens, rollerball pens and the humble ballpoint pen are all fine, and depending on whether they are water-soluble or not can achieve a range of marks. Water-soluble ink can blur effectively when it is touched with water.

Black watercolour is slower drying than ink, so is more forgiving to handle and will offer subtle veils of tone, and you can create a number of tones swiftly just by diluting.

Brushes are useful drawing tools, too, and can be used to apply a range of washes. Art shops generally stock a wide range: you might start with soft-bristled rounds (the most common type, with a pointed tip) as these move fluidly over paper, but do experiment with fine oriental brushes, which are good for controlled lines, and even flat brushes or square-ended brushes for bold sketches.

Miscellaneous equipment

You will also need an eraser, a knife or sharpener, a plastic bottle for water if you are not sketching at home, and a bag in which to keep everything while you are on the move.

Starting at home

The idea of just sitting down and starting to sketch out of the blue, even in your own living room, is a little daunting. It helps if you begin with the ordinary, so set aside a short set time, say half an hour, to take yourself on a brief visual journey through your home and to sketch something that attracts you. Don't worry at this stage about composition or design; try to focus on a corner with a few objects that have simple shapes. Feel free in a sketchbook to simplify and edit a scene, or (when occasion demands) investigate something very thoroughly.

To isolate an image imagine you are looking through a camera lens; just as you would when taking a photo, aim to avoid the distraction of the rest of the room. One way of making this easier is to make a cut-out viewfinder from a piece of card.

When you start a sketch you should have an aim in mind, but this often changes: you may find youself embarking on a sketch only as a means of jotting down information to find that it ends up being a stimulus for a large painting.

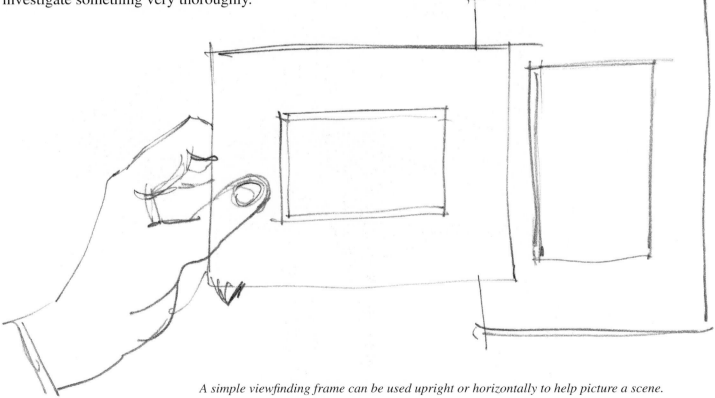

A simple viewfinding frame can be used upright or horizontally to help picture a scene.

The living room

Here, I have chosen to sketch a corner of a table, a chair, and the suggestion of a plant, using a 2B pencil.

Mark out very lightly the important points of the general structure. The plant pot's height, the shape and height of the chair and the surface of the table all need to be gently established from the start. To get some sense of scale, use a pencil held vertically at arm's length to 'measure' the proportions of one item in relation to another. Indoors you are never dealing with huge distances, but the size and angle of the table edge and the slight enlarging of the nearer handle create a sense of depth.

I used a touch of hatching to give the cushion solidity and to indicate the curve on the leg of the table. The sketch has no edges – what you leave out is just as important as what you put in.

The kitchen

The kitchen is often the heart of the house, and signs of life make for lively sketching. I found plenty of things to sketch in my own and friends' kitchens.

In the sketch of the Aga all the tea towels drying and the array of kitchen utensils hanging overhead added interest, and the brickwork gave the sketch a strong structure.

This was sketched with an HB pencil, the underlying fine lines put in first with very light pressure to give a skeleton to work upon. Personally, I don't mind these showing through the final sketch – the skill of a clean contour line can be honed later. Again, proportions can be assessed with the help of a pencil held up to the scene. As the lines are mainly horizontal and vertical, like a grid, the rest fitted over quite easily. I shaded the areas in shadow, such as the side of the cooker, with crosshatching.

In another kitchen I was interested in the view out towards the hall, and wanted to include the drying herbs hanging over the doorway. I used a waterproof rollerball and ink diluted to make a wash for the shadows, pushing the ink wash around with a brush. Don't plunge into the darkest shadows first, wait until you are more confident in judging the different relationships of tone: work from the lightest wash and build up into the darkest areas, in this case under the door. In this sketch there is an element of perspective to take into account; this will be tackled later (see pages 24–5).

Work rooms

I drew my studio and a friend's music room, but you might just as easily focus on the washing machine, your desk, a wall of tools or the interior of a garden shed.

I chose a very soft charcoal pencil to suggest the piano against the window, and only barely hinted at what can be seen outside the window.

My studio was a lightning sketch with brush and watercolour. It was looking relatively tidy and so speed was both my choice and a knowledge that it would not look so neat for long! (Having said that, the messy evidence of people also makes interesting sketching.)

The bedroom

A bedroom scene gives a very intimate view of the owner, so look for little signs that are intriguing and attractive. Here, the dressing gown is the focal point, the bed itself left as a simple shape, although I paid attention to the pillows and how they sat. It took only a few lines to indicate the gathers. The paleness of the bed linen is emphasized by its contrast to the bedhead.

Using a brush and grey watercolour gives a wobbly, fluid line, which is the major difference in exhanging your pencil for wet materials. The light was going, so I had to put a spurt on and I think this sketch benefits from a casual treatment – perhaps the essence of successful sketching is to look hard and give the study some thought, so that less is more when it comes to the actual physical drawing.

This very quick sketch of the chest of drawers was made with an art pen, brush and water. Soften lines by just running the brush against the line. The effect can also be useful for covering mistakes: when you abandon the pencil you also lose the ability to erase. But it's only a sketch, so plunge in and experiment.

For the sketch on the left I used charcoal for a darker-shadowed, less defined look, adding a few final highlights by erasing. The sketch below is a watercolour, noticeably more fluid and with more marked and yet more subtle degrees of light and shade.

Experimenting with tone is also a chance to expand into different materials and have fun with the variety of possible effects. The sketch on the previous page was done with a 2B pencil, the first degree of shading done by hatching, and darker areas emphasized with cross-hatching.

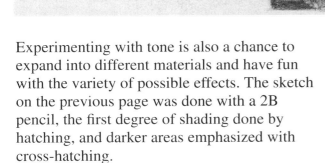

The large windows in this grand London house
let in wonderful shafts of light from both sides,
creating interesting areas of light and shadow on
the floor. The columns are a good example of
how shading works to depict a curved surface.
The shade is indicated by hatching and as the
paper was very smooth the pencil slid with ease
over the surface.

The conservatory was a perfect place to show the effect of light on an interior. I used pencil for the architectural structure and for some of the areas of tone. A further ink wash worked best for the looser shadows. Be bold in leaving the paper white for the lightest zones.

Details and interesting corners

As you observe and sketch, you will probably be diverted by delightful groupings of all the personal paraphernalia of a house's inhabitants. Kitchen utensils, china, plants, packets of detergent, they are all made up of those basic shapes discussed on pages 26–27, so you are well equipped to tackle interesting corners.

If you need to practise ellipses, then something like the delicate perfume bottles on the bath-room shelf would be an ideal subject. I was inspired by the faceted transparent glass and the unusual shapes. I chose a 2B pencil because the pattern of the objects and the way they overlapped was suitable for treatment in line only. The basket's woven texture was just suggested by sharp repeated lines to indicate the overall pattern – there was no need to fill it all in. Notice how the bottles on the top shelf have narrow ellipses and those on the lower shelf are rounder because they are further below my eye level. I like the way the tap and sink slide out of the picture.

Another shelf with a set of baskets and patterned jugs was an opportunity for sketching in pen, ink and wash. Both sketches demanded I look closely at the shapes *between* the objects. These 'negative shapes' are as important as the more obvious shapes of the objects themselves – turning the sketch upside down will help you see

them not just as background white paper. The relationship of one shape against another becomes important, so you are not putting each down unrelated, like a shopping list. The perfume bottles (above) are another good example of how attention to the proportion of these negative shapes makes it an airy and open

design, echoing the transparency of the bottles. The pen and wash (far right) has less area of negative shape and the feel is much more dense. If you focus on both sets of shapes when sketching, the chances are you will produce a better balanced drawing.

This very modest plant study is a mono-chromatic watercolour sketch in a limited range of tones. The negative shape of the dark leaves behind the fern reveal the light side of the pot. I had to be careful to remember to leave the paper bare for the lightest areas.

The very flowing study of Edwardian lighting in a Paris restaurant was made from high up, as I planned to sketch the whole scene below. But time ran out so I resorted to a camera to record the rest.

It was such a challenge constructing the shape of the rather grand woven chair with the round pillow to make it look three-dimensional and textural that I ran out of steam and just suggested the rest of the room. Using pen and ink, I let the ink run all over the place, as it was sketched on hot-pressed smooth paper.

Sketches often remain unfinished, but an incomplete sketch is as valuable as a finished one. I am rather relieved that I didn't get to put all the detail in, as you get the idea of the hall, stairs and hat stand well enough. This was done in conte pencil.

Gridding

Sketches can be records in their own right or the first stage in the development of a larger, more carefully worked image.

To scale up a sketch for transfer on to a larger paper or canvas you can either draw a grid of squares on to your original or draw a grid on to an acetate overlay. Draw a similar grid (i.e. with the same amount of squares) on to your new sheet, enlarging it as much as necessary to correspond to the final size of picture. You can then refer to the grid over the original sketch to plot the outlines square by square on your final drawing or painting.

To conclude

A sketchbook is the perfect place to improve your drawing skills and your powers of observation. Your very personal immediate impression, may be just a few essential strokes, could be the inspiration for further work. When looking back through sketchbooks, they are are also a valuable social and personal record.